FOR THE OLDER BEGINNER

PERFORMANCE BOOK

BOOK 1

ACCELERATED

PIANO

Adventure® *by Nancy and Randall Faber*

CONTENTS

Backpacking

Moderately

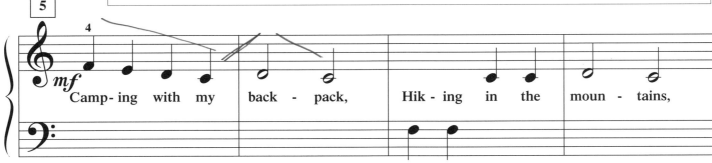

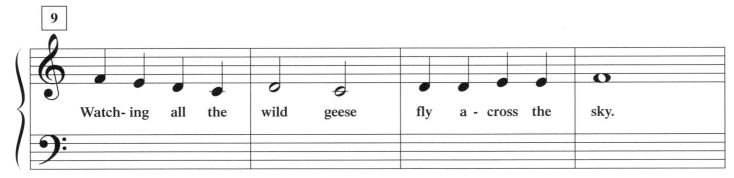

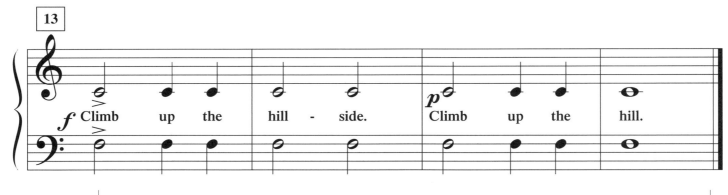

Teacher Duet: (Student plays *1 octave higher*. Teacher pedals.)

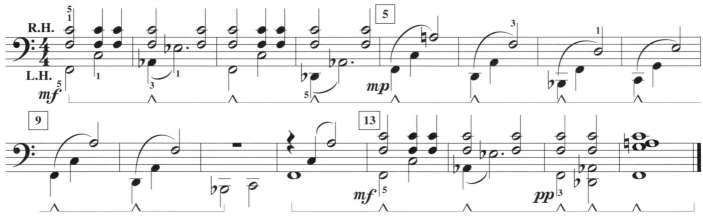

Rhythm Check: Are you counting to 3 for each ♩.?

Alouette

Traditional French folk song
arranged

Cheerfully

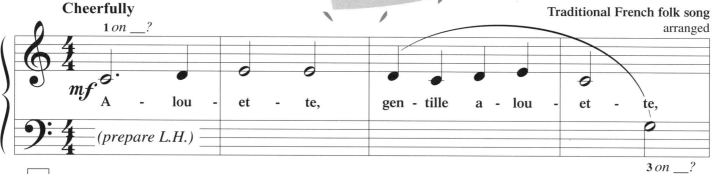

1 on ___?

mf

A - lou - et - te, gen - tille a - lou - et - te,

(prepare L.H.)

3 on ___?

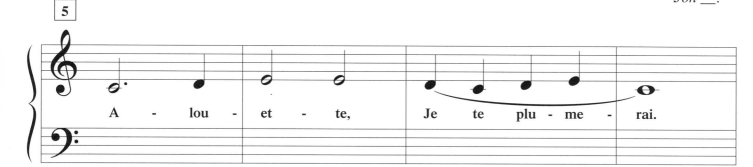

5

A - lou - et - te, Je te plu - me - rai.

9

Je te plu - me - rai la tête, Je te plu - me - rai la tête,

Repeat the first two lines to end the piece.

13

f Et la tête, Et la tête, Oh!_____

DISCOVERY

Name the notes aloud for this piece.

Teacher Duet: (Student plays *1 octave higher*)

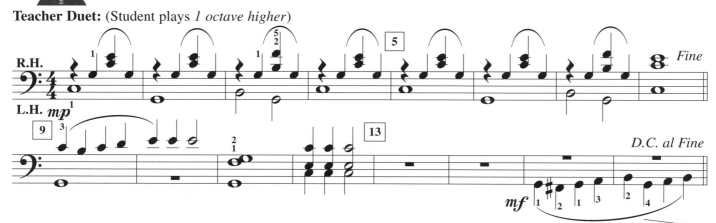

R.H.

L.H. *mp*

Fine

D.C. al Fine

mf

207

Hand Position Check:
Are you playing with a
rounded hand position
and firm fingertips?

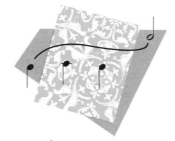

Theme by Mozart

(from *Sonata in A Major,* K. 331)

Wolfgang Amadeus Mozart
(1756–1791, Austria)
arranged

Rather slowly

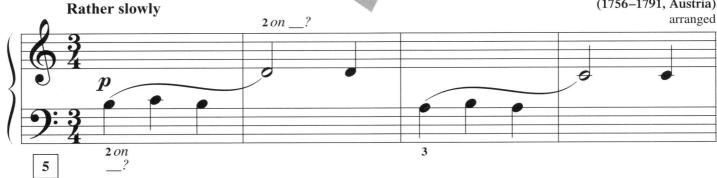

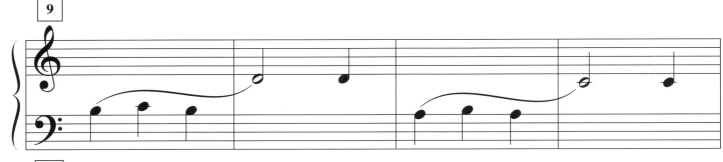

DISCOVERY

Circle the **repeated notes** in this piece.

Teacher Duet: (Student plays *1 octave higher*)

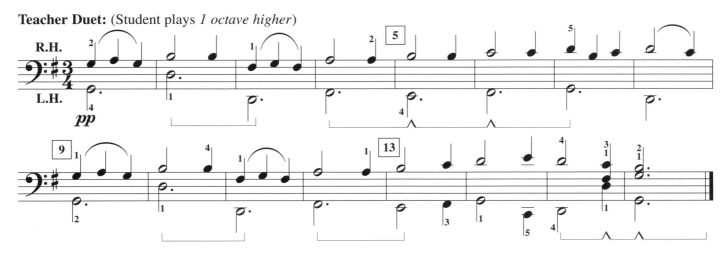

4

Rhythm Check: Tap the rhythm of *measure 1* before playing.

Party Time

Traditional
arranged

DISCOVERY Where are *measures 1–4* repeated in this piece?

Teacher Duet: (Student plays *1 octave higher*)

(*Allegro* is the Italian word for fast and lively.)

 **Allegro**

Mauro Giuliani
(1781–1829, Italy)
arranged

Cheerfully

1 *on* ___?

f

1 *on* ___?

5

p

Teacher Duet: (Student plays *1 octave higher*)

R.H.

L.H.

mf-pp on repeat

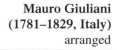 **Boogie in 3rds**

Fast

2 *on* ___?

3

f

5

4 *on* ___?

Teacher Duet: (Student plays *1 octave higher*)

R.H.

L.H.

mf

Carousel Melody

Moderately fast

DISCOVERY Name the two intervals played by the R.H.

Teacher Duet: (Student plays *1 octave higher*)

 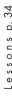

Showboat

Cheerfully

1 on __?

mf Come take the riv - er show- boat! Folks, there is real - ly no boat

3 on __?

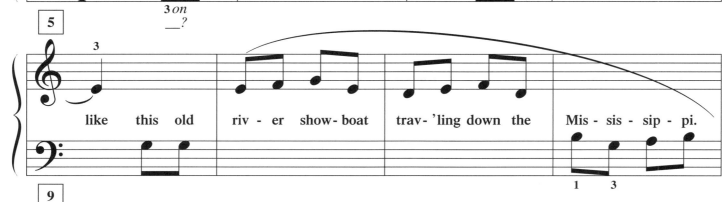

5

like this old riv - er show- boat trav- 'ling down the Mis - sis - sip - pi.

9

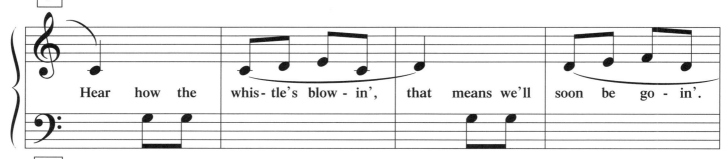

Hear how the whis- tle's blow - in', that means we'll soon be go - in'.

13

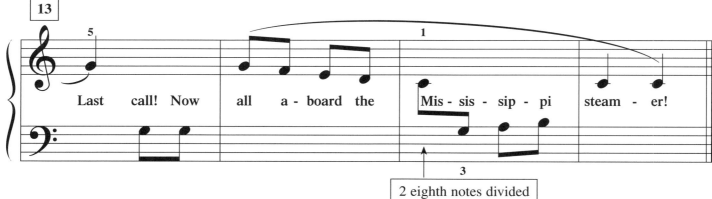

Last call! Now all a - board the Mis - sis - sip - pi steam - er!

2 eighth notes divided
between the hands.

Teacher Duet: (Student plays *1 octave higher*)

FF1

Reading Check: Circle all the **3rds (skips)** in this piece.

Simple Gifts

Traditional Shaker melody
arranged

Rather slowly

'Tis the gift to be sim-ple, 'tis the gift to be free, 'tis the gift to come down where we ought to be. And when we find our-selves in the place just right, 'twill be in the val - ley of love and de - light.

DISCOVERY On which beat does this piece begin? **beat 1   beat 2   beat 3   beat 4** *(circle one)*

Teacher Duet: (Student plays *1 octave higher*)

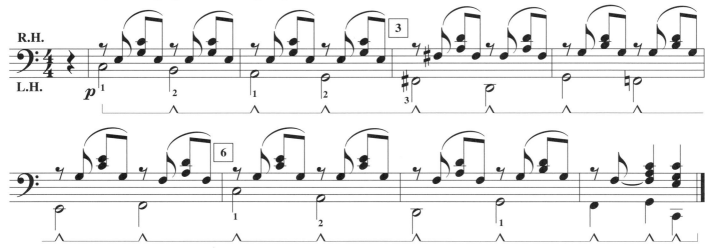

The Spanish Guitar

Francesco Molino
(1775–1847, Spain)
arranged

Moving along gently

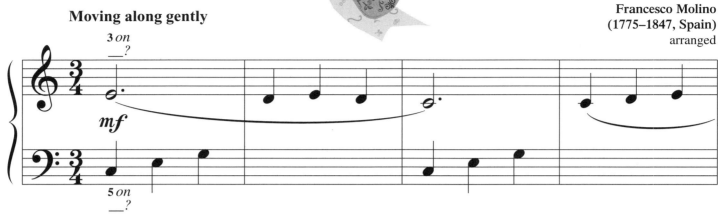

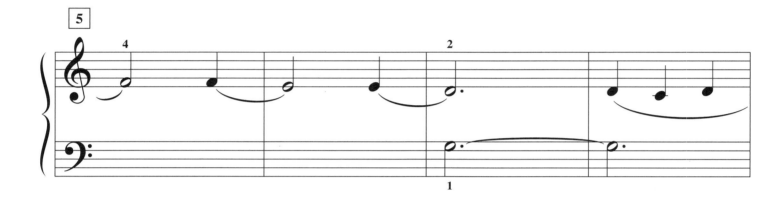

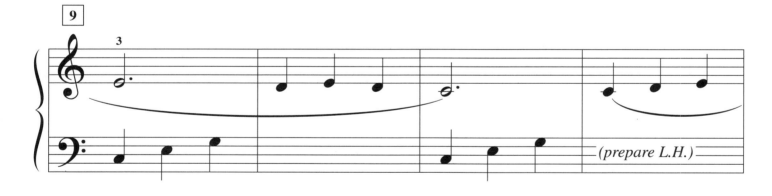

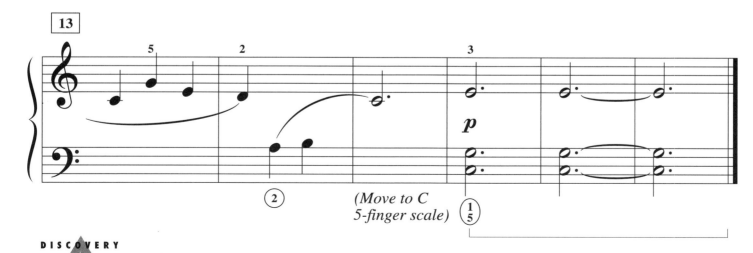

DISCOVERY

Point out two **ties** in this piece to your teacher.

Clock Tower Bells
(Theme and Variation)

Traditional theme
arranged

Theme

Moderately

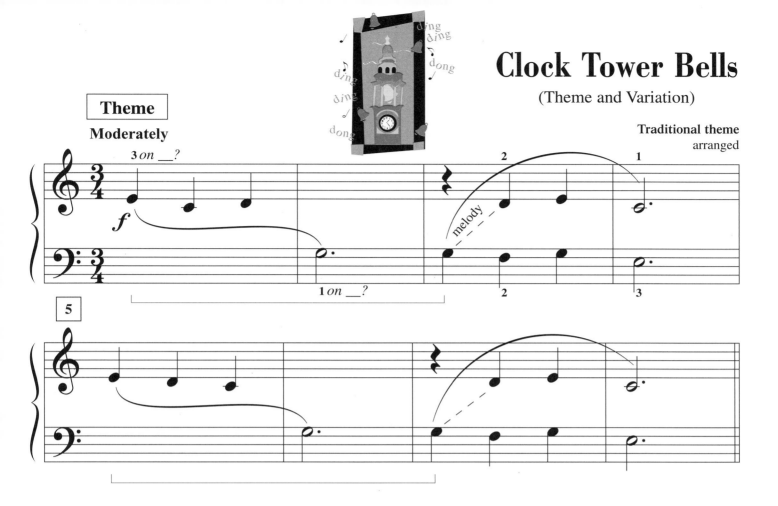

Variation

A *variation* may alter the theme in different ways: rhythm, notes, dynamics, etc.

Lessons p. 44

1207

Wrist Check: Are your wrists
relaxed as you play *staccato*?

Strike Up the Band!

Lyric by Andrew B. Sterling
Music by Charles B. Ward
arranged

With pep

Strike up the band, here comes a sail - or.

Teacher Duet: (Student plays *1 octave higher*)

FF1

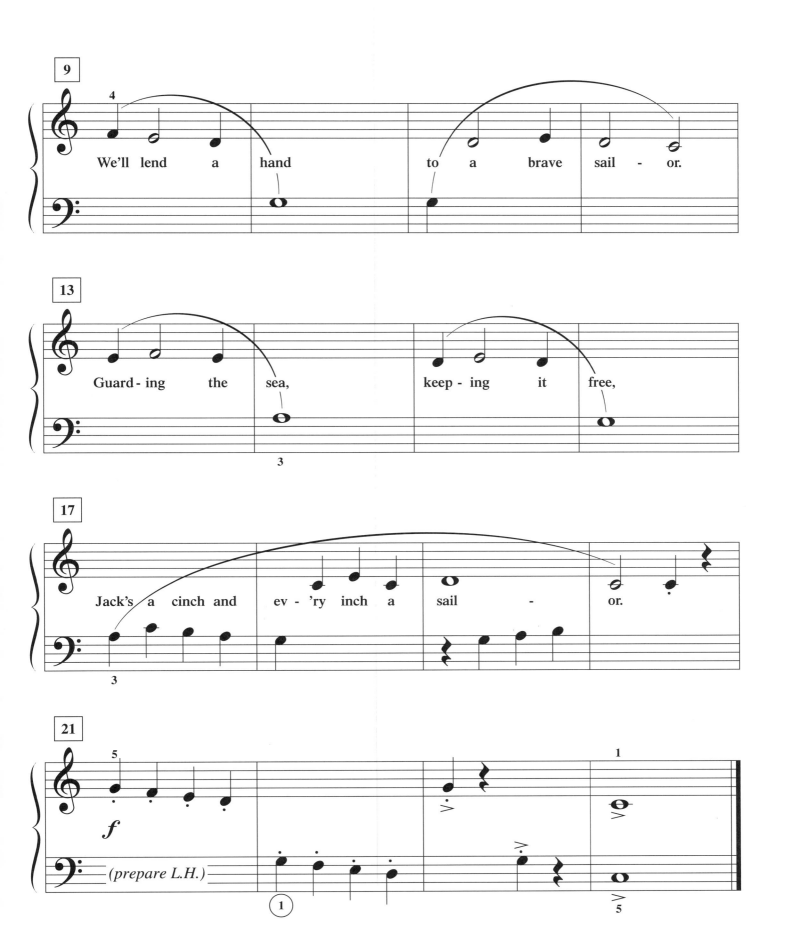

DISCOVERY

How does the introduction (*measures 1–4*) differ from the ending (*measures 21–24*)?

Sound Check: Are you observing
the *f*, *mf*, and *p* signs in the music?

La Cinquantaine*

Gabriel Marie
(1852–1928, France)
arranged

1st and 2nd endings
Play the 1st ending and take the repeat. Then play
the 2nd ending, skipping over the 1st ending.

*The Golden Wedding (pronounced Lah SEHN-kun-tehn)

Teacher Duet: (Student plays *1 octave higher*)

Hand Position Check: Are you playing with a rounded hand position and firm fingertips?

Reveille*

U.S. Army Bugle Call
arranged

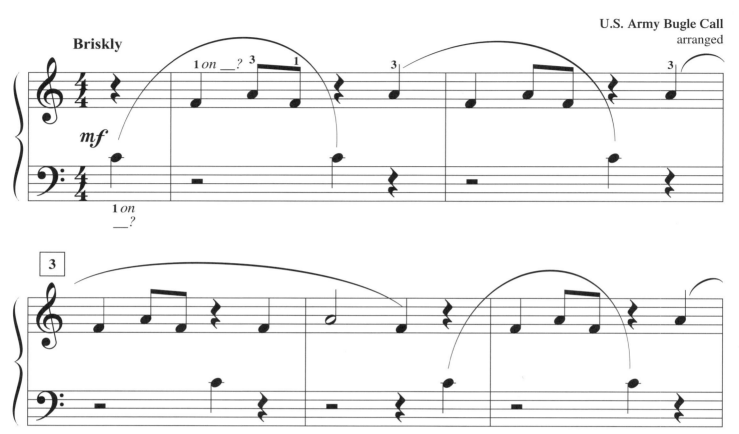

*pronounced REV-eh-lee

Teacher Duet: (Student plays *1 octave higher*)

FF12

DISCOVERY

This piece uses only three letter names. Name them: ____, ____, and ____

The Handbell Choir

Secondo - Teacher Part

Cornelius Gurlitt

Not too fast

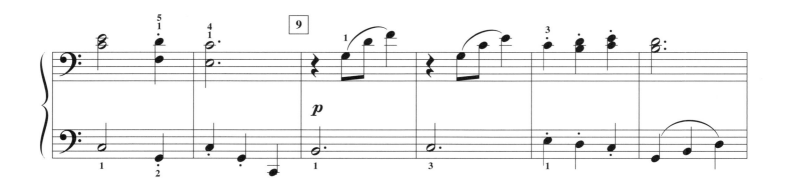

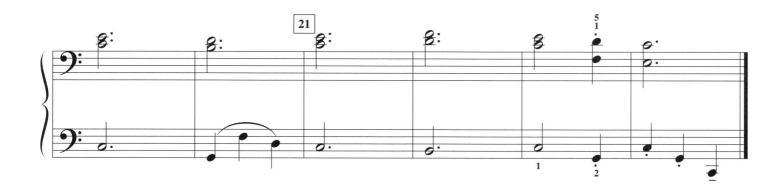

FF1

The *primo* is the top part in a 4-hand piano duet.
The primo is usually written with two treble clefs.

The *secondo* is the lower part in a 4-hand piano duet.
The secondo is usually written with two bass clefs.

The Handbell Choir
Primo - Student Part

Cornelius Gurlitt
(1820–1901, Germany)
original form

Lessons p. 56

D I S C O V E R Y   Where is the **1st phrase** repeated in the piece? *measure* _____

Where is the **2nd phrase** repeated in the piece? *measure* _____

Painting With Pastels

My pastels are ready by the easel.

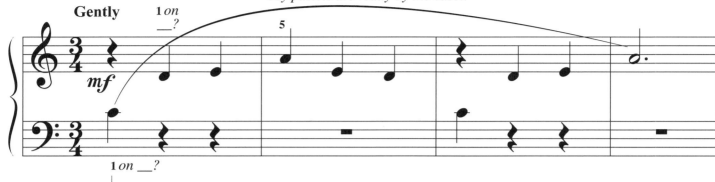

Gently   *mf*   **1** *on* __?

1 *on* __?

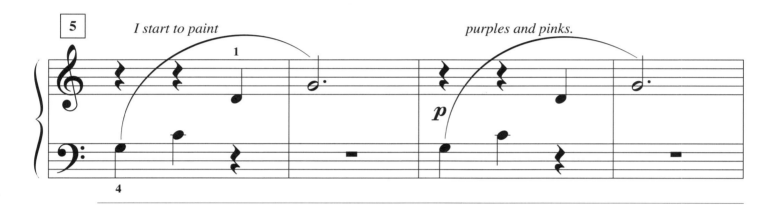

5   *I start to paint*   *purples and pinks.*   *p*   **4**

9   *These colors mingle with blues and greens.*   *mf*

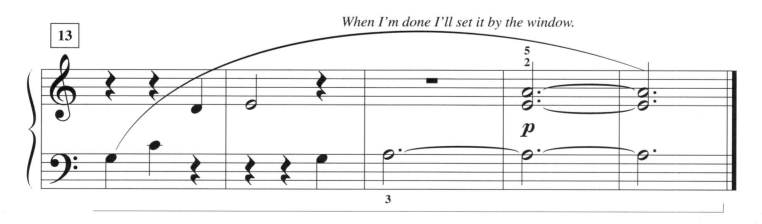

13   *When I'm done I'll set it by the window.*   *p*   **3**

DISCOVERY This piece has 3 different **fourths**. Write the note names of each.

_____ to _____   _____ to _____   _____ to _____

FF1

A Merry March

Cornelius Gurlitt
(1820–1901, Germany)
original form

DISCOVERY Find and circle each **4th** in this piece.
Don't forget to look for L.H. 4ths.

(duet by Faber and Faber)

Teacher Duet: (Student plays *as written*)

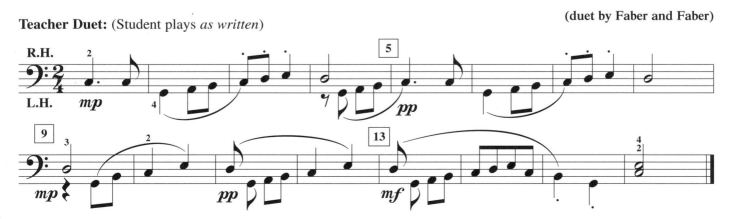

Lessons p. 63

This piece is in **ABA form** with a 4-measure
introduction and a 4-measure ending (called a *coda*).

- Label the **introduction**, **A section**, **B section**,
  return of the **A section**, and **coda** in the music.

Square Dance

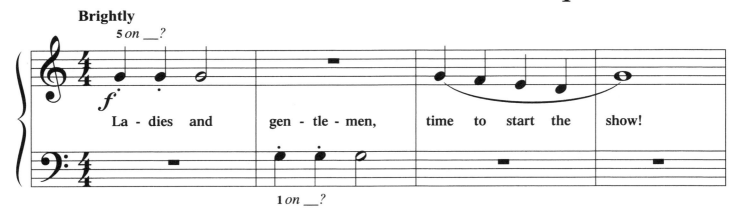

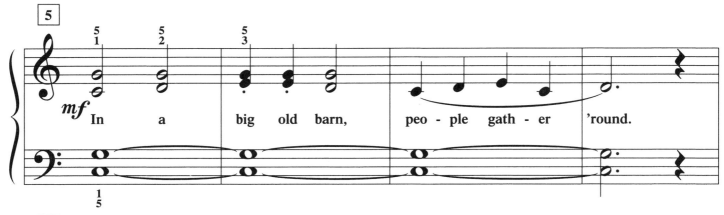

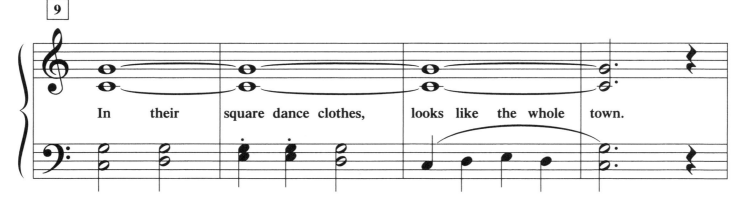

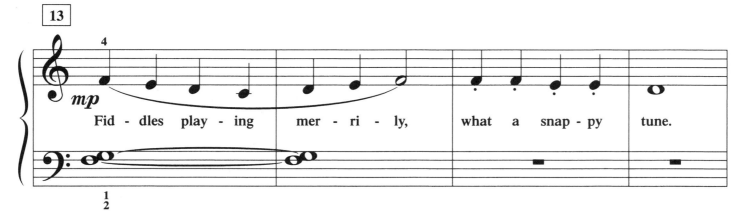

22

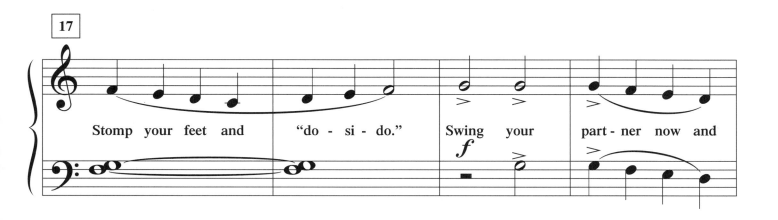

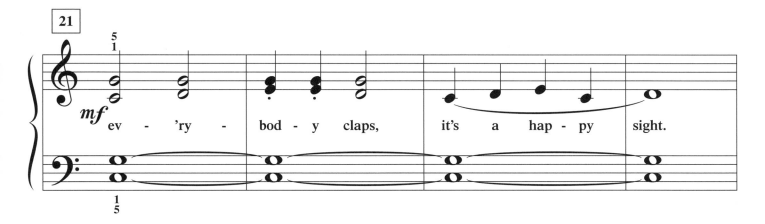

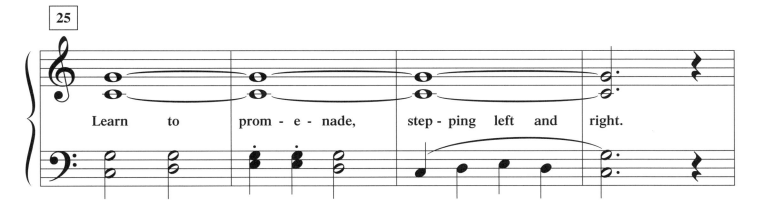

 DISCOVERY

What interval is played by the right hand in the final measure? _____

Greensleeves

Gently moving

English folk song
arranged

A - las, my love____ you do me wrong____ to cast me off____ dis - cour - teous - ly. And I have

Teacher Duet: (Student plays *1 octave higher*)

R.H.

L.H. *p* *with pedal*

Note: Students may play the familiar ♩. ♪ ♩ rhythm in this piece, if desired.

FF1

DISCOVERY

On what beat does this piece begin?   **beat 1**   **beat 2**   **beat 3**   *(circle one)*

Snake Dance

Traditional melody
arranged

Teacher Duet: (Student plays the L.H. *1 octave higher*)

FF12

Play *Snake Dance* with the L.H. 1 octave *lower* than written.

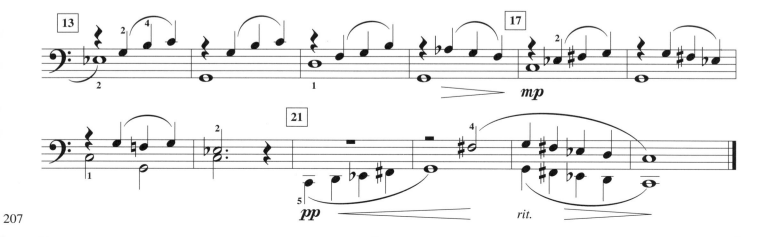

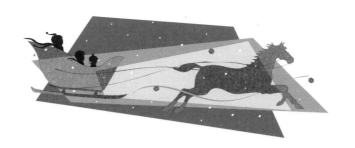

Left Hand Check: Is your L.H. rocking gently back and forth for the 8th notes?

Horse and Sleigh

Trotting briskly

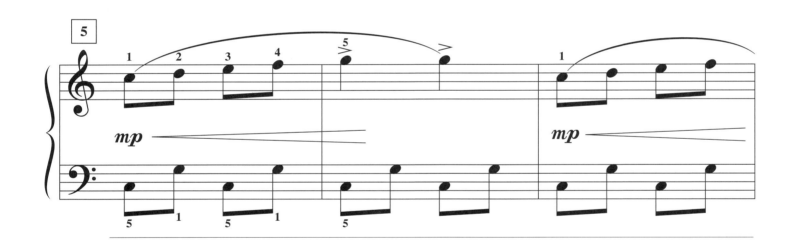

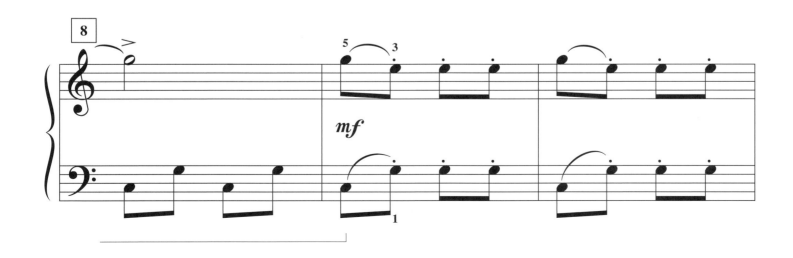

FF1

Repeat from the beginning, playing the R.H. 1 octave HIGHER.

Put a ✔ under each measure where the L.H. plays only **tonic** and **dominant notes**.

207

A *sonatina* is a piece for piano or other musical instrument that usually has two or three *movements* (large sections). Notice that each movement has a character and tempo (speed) of its own. The performer should pause between movements, and the audience should wait until the end of the sonatina to applaud.

Miniature Sonatina

Joseph Kuffner
(1776–1856, Germany)
arranged

FF1

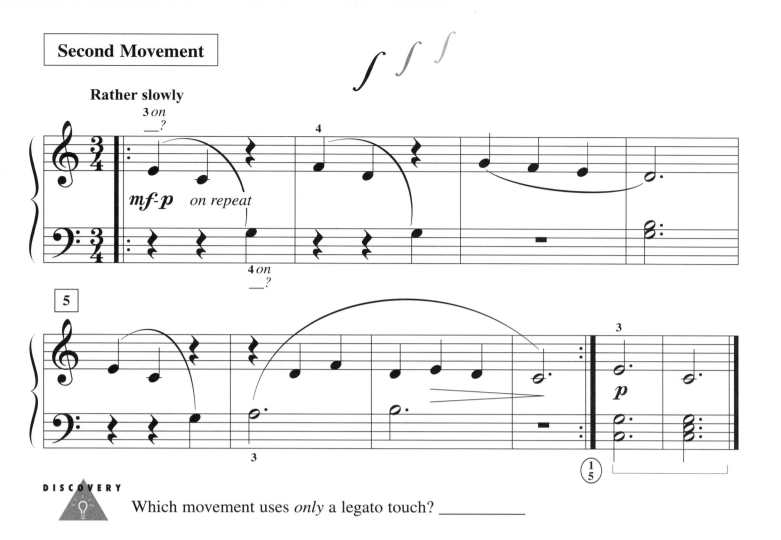

Second Movement

DISCOVERY

Which movement uses *only* a legato touch? _____

Teacher Duets

First Movement (Student plays *1 octave higher*)

Second Movement (Student plays *1 octave higher*)

fermata—Hold this note longer than usual.

For He's a Jolly Good Fellow

Traditional
arranged

Fast and fun

1 *on* __?
3 *on* __?
5 *on* __?

mf For he's a jol - ly good fel - low, for

he's a jol - ly good fel - low, for

L.H. ② *over*

(cross L.H. over R.H.)

he's a jol - ly good fel - low, which *f*

R.H. no - bo - dy can de - ny._____ Which *mp*

no - bo - dy can de - ny,_____ which

cross ② *over the thumb*

FF1

DISCOVERY

Label the **A section**, **B section**, and return of the **A section** in this piece.

1207

33

The San Francisco Trolley

G 5-Finger Scale

Sound Check: Circle the abbreviations *cresc.* and *dim.* in this piece. What do they mean?

On   the   track,   hear the trol-ley

FF12

DISCOVERY

What note does the L.H. play that is *not* in the G pentascale? _____

March of the English Guard

_____ **5-Finger Scale**

Jeremiah Clarke
(1659–1707, England)
arranged

Proudly marching

1 on __?

f

1 on __?

3

1

Teacher Duet: (Student plays *1 octave higher*)

R.H.

L.H. *mf*

5

7

9

p

11

14

mf

DISCOVERY

Write a **I** or **V⁷** under each chord in this piece.

x

Write a **I** or **V^7** under each chord in this piece.

x

Mr. McGill

Combining C and G 5-Finger Scales

Note: The teacher may wish to first clap the rhythm of *measures 1–2* and have the student imitate.

Lively

mf

Mis - ter Mc - Gill____ lived high on a hill,____ you can be sure that he lives there still.____ Ev - er - y day____ the

neigh - bors all say,____ he'd sing tunes at his pi - a - no this way.____

L.H. moves quickly

"Doo - wah, doo - wah boop she - bop!____ Boop she - bop!____

38

FF12

Label the **A section**, **B section**, and return of the **A section** in this piece.

Piano Repertoire List

Piano pieces that you have learned well and can readily play for family and friends make up your *repertoire* (pronounced REP-er-twar).

Make a repertoire list by writing the title and composer of favorite pieces you have learned. Enjoy playing your repertoire!

Title	**Composer**	✔ if memorized
		☐
		☐
		☐
		☐
		☐
		☐
		☐
		☐
		☐
		☐
		☐
		☐
		☐
		☐
		☐
		☐
		☐
		☐
		☐
		☐
		☐

Note: Pieces in this book are by Faber & Faber unless otherwise indicated.